I0489589

Wealthy Lotus

You're amazing
just the
way you
are.

www.ingramcontent.com/pod-product-compliance
Lightning Source LLC
Chambersburg PA
CBHW081730220526
45468CB00008B/2045
* 9 7 8 1 7 2 3 9 6 9 1 4 0 *